THE BARTENDER'S GUIDE TO MOCKTAILS

THE BARTENDER'S GUIDE TO
MOCKTAILS

CREATE ON-TREND, NON-ALCOHOLIC DRINKS WITH ATTITUDE

CONTENTS

THE RISE OF THE MOCKTAIL

The word 'mocktail' is a marriage of 'mock' and 'cocktail'. While there is no recorded date for when these non-alcoholic drinks first became popular, the word itself was coined in 1979 in an advertisement for a glassware brand. The concept of mocktails must, however, predate this. As long as people have drunk in bars, bartenders will have needed to provide tempting libations for any customers who wished to steer clear of the hard stuff.

Non-alcoholic beverages became more popular than ever during the Prohibition years in the US (1920–1933). This led to the creation of the 'soda jerk', a person who operated soda fountains in drugstores throughout the US. The Soda Jerk would create drinks in a tall glass, using flavoured syrups mixed with carbonated water and topped with one or two scoops of ice cream. These were served with a long-handled spoon and drinking straws – this trend reached its height in the 1940s.

While outlawing alcohol during Prohibition negatively affected the previously burgeoning US cocktail culture, it also created a renaissance for temperance drinks. These concoctions could be time-consuming to make and surprisingly complex. As a result, people started to experiment with more interesting ingredients including shrubs, syrups and fresh fruit, a trend that we are seeing again in the creation of modern-day cocktails and mocktails.

Today, the mocktail revolution is just behind the cocktail revival. Bartenders are spending as much time creating mocktails with complex flavour profiles as they spend creating cocktails. There is clearly a large market for quality mocktails and this is likely to be driven by a mainstream interest in living a healthy lifestyle and cutting out processed ingredients and excess sugar from our diet. Good-quality non-alcoholic offerings also appeal to a

broad range of people – from pregnant women to athletes and many in between – so it is worth planning the creation of your mocktails in the same way as you would your alcoholic drinks.

This book will give you ideas for making mocktails at home or in the bar, and can also be used as a guide for experimenting. Just remember that the process of making drinks can be as much fun as drinking them!

INGREDIENTS

Any mixed drink relies on an appropriate combination of ingredients to endow it with mixology magic. There is a wide variety of ingredients suitable for mocktails – shown below are the main categories that you will encounter in this book, and that you can use as you start to experiment with your own mocktails.

JUICES

Juices can come in a number of forms, ranging from freshly squeezed juices and store-bought brands to pulps and fruit nectars. Whichever you choose for your mocktails, remember that freshly squeezed juice will give you the purest tasting experience and the best-quality drinks. You can make your own juices at home using an electric juicer, a Mexican Elbow squeezer (see below left) or even just by giving the fruit sections a good squeeze by hand. Freshly squeezed juice will need to be strained to remove any bits.

SYRUPS

Syrups, a combination of sugar and water, are used all over the world by mixologists, baristas and chefs both to sweeten and add flavour to their creations. There is a huge variety of brands that create flavoured syrups such as cola, vanilla, bubble gum and rosemary, but it is also easy to create your own. Some of the mocktail recipes here tell you how to make your own syrups; others use shop-bought syrups. There is also a practical guide to making your own syrup on page 113.

SHRUBS

A shrub is a slightly acidic liquid traditionally made with fruit, sugar and vinegar. The name 'shrub' is derived from an Arabic word meaning 'to drink'. The idea of shrubs originates from the creation of medicinal cordials in the 15th century. Shrubs were also popular in colonial America, then mixed with cool water to provide a pick-me-up on hot days, as well as during America's Prohibition era, providing a tasty, thirst-quenching beverage with no alcohol.

A proper shrub has a flavour that is both sweet and tart, so it stimulates the appetite while also quenching thirst. Shrubs are easy to make at home, and for mocktail lovers they're also quite versatile. If you are prepared for a summer of shrub-making, you can start with strawberries when they come into season, and move through the berries and fruits as they mature over the summer. Some of the mocktail recipes here tell you how to make your own shrubs. There is also a practical guide to making your own shrub on page 149.

TEA AND COFFEE

Tea has been used for centuries as a delicious beverage, both hot and cold. With a huge variety of teas including bagged, loose-leaf, herbal and even matcha power, there is a never-ending list of possible flavours. There are many uses for tea within mocktails, including infusions, chilled tea and tea syrups.

Coffee has grown in popularity as an ingredient in mixed drinks over the past few years. There are many ways to use coffee in mocktails, ranging from using the beans as a garnish or using iced coffee as an ingredient to create coffee-flavoured syrups. When creating your own flavours you can use both the bean and

ground coffee depending on the style and flavour profile you are aiming to achieve.

PURÉES

A purée is an easy way to enhance a mocktail with fruity flavours without needing to muddle fruit directly into your mixed drink. To make your own purée at home, prepare your fruit and place it in a blender or food processor with sugar and lemon juice and process for around 30 seconds. Pour into a fine sieve set over a bowl, press the liquid through the sieve with a rubber spatula and discard the solids. You can make a purée using any fruit or vegetable with a high juice content.

HERBS AND SPICES

When bartenders get creative and design new mixed drinks, many techniques and ingredients are 'borrowed' from the kitchen. One of these includes the use of herbs and spices. Ingredients such as cinnamon, basil, cardamom and lavender have found their way into the bartender's repertoire to create delicious mocktails. There are also many classic, internationally recognised drinks that use fresh mint. There are many ways to use these fresh, fragrant ingredients such as in infusions, syrups and shrubs.

GLASSWARE

How you present and serve your drinks is crucial in any form of mixology. You need to serve a mocktail in the appropriate glass – the size, shape and style all have an impact on the perception and enjoyment of the drink. Here are some of the classic glasses that you will likely have in your collection, although be aware that there are no set rules.

MARTINI GLASS

The most iconic of all mixed drink glasses, the conical martini glass emerged with the Art Deco movement. The glass has a low, wide bowl and the long stem is perfect for chilled drinks as it keeps people's hands from inadvertently warming the cocktail.

HIGHBALL GLASS

Sometimes also known as a Collins or Slim Jim glass, these glasses are perfect for serving drinks with a higher portion of liquid. The highball glass is versatile enough to be a substitute for the similarly shaped, but slightly larger, Collins glass.

ROCKS GLASS

The rocks glass, also known as a lowball or an old-fashioned glass, is a short, squat tumbler and is great for serving any short mocktails. It is also the perfect glass where simple drinks garnishes are required.

FLUTE

The tall, thin, tapered design of the flute glass reduces the surface area of a sparkling mocktail and so helps to keep the bubbles in the drink for longer. The flute has now largely replaced the old-fashioned coupe glass for serving sparkling mocktails.

COUPETTE GLASS

The coupette or margarita glass, as its second name implies, was designed specifically for serving margaritas. It is ideal for any frozen, blended mocktail recipes.

COUPE GLASS

This wide-rimmed glass is good for serving sparkling drinks. It was once the glass of choice for champagne but works perfectly for sparkling mocktails, too. Legend has it that the glass is modelled on the breast of Marie Antoinette.

SNIFTER GLASS

The bowl-shaped snifter glass, also referred to as a balloon, invites drinkers to cradle the drink in their hands, warming the contents of the glass, so it is a good option for warmed mocktails, such as a mulled mock wine. The aroma of the drink is held in the glass, allowing you to breathe in the drink's aroma before sipping it.

HURRICANE GLASS

This pear-shaped glass pays homage to the hurricane lamp. It was the glass used to create the New Orleans rum-based cocktail, the Hurricane. It's also an excellent glass for a variety of frozen and blended mocktails.

PITCHER

Although not strictly a glass, a pitcher or jug is a great addition to your mocktail glassware. Mocktails are perfect drinks to be shared with friends and family and a good pitcher is an easy way to ensure there is enough for everyone.

WINE GLASS

The style of wine glass we see today is closely related to the Jacobite glass used to drink wine from the 1700s onwards, on which each Freemason lodge had their own design engraved. Today there is a huge variety of wine glasses, most off them stemmed to keep the drink cold.

EQUIPMENT

The equipment you have in your home bar will depend on whether you are someone who likes all the latest gadgets, or whether you are happy making do with some basic options. There is no limit to the amount of bar equipment available, but you don't need lots of kit to make most of the drinks in this book. Here are the essential tools of the trade.

MEASURES AND JIGGERS

A jigger is a drink-maker's basic measuring tool and is essential for crafting the perfect blend of ingredients. You can get a steel jigger with clear measurement markings so you can pour out measures easily and accurately.

BAR SPOON

A proper bar spoon has a small bowl (always 5 ml/1 tsp) and a long handle that allows you to muddle, mix, layer and stir with ease. Spoons come in a variety of lengths and widths, and a stylish bar spoon is an attractive addition to any bartender's kit.

SHAKER

Most contemporary shakers are made from steel as steel doesn't tarnish readily and doesn't conduct heat easily – this is useful when making chilled mocktails as the ice cools the mocktail rather than the shaker. Most standard shakers, known as cobbler shakers, come with a built-in strainer, but if you're using a Boston or Parisian shaker then you'll need to use a separate strainer.

STRAINER

A Hawthorne strainer is an essential tool to prevent ice and other ingredients being poured into your glass. Some mocktails need to be double-strained so even if there is a strainer in your cocktail shaker, you'll still need a separate fine strainer in your bar collection. Another style of strainer is the julep strainer, used to hold ice back in stirred drinks.

MIXING GLASS OR BEAKER

Any vessel that holds about 500 ml/1 pint of liquid can be used for mixing drinks. It is good to have a mixing glass with a spout or ridged rim so that you can stop ice from slipping into the glass, but this is not vital as a strainer can be used. Mixing beakers are increasingly popular nowadays, and are usually made of glass or crystal.

MUDDLER

For mashing up citrus fruit or crushing herbs, you need a muddler. This is a chunky wooden, plastic or metal tool with a rounded end and it can also be used to make cracked ice. You can mash fruit or crush herbs with a mortar and pestle, but the advantage of a muddler is that it can be used directly in the mixing glass.

JUICER

A traditional, ridged half-lemon shape on a saucer will work perfectly well for juicing small amounts. There is also a citrus spout that screws into a lemon or lime and is useful for obtaining tiny amounts of juice. Mechanical or electric presses are great for large amounts of juice, but are not essential in a home bar. A cheaper option is called a Mexican Elbow – these work by pressing the juice out of citrus fruits.

OTHER EQUIPMENT

Other items you might need in your home-bar equipment are olive sticks, blender, tongs, an ice bucket, a chopping board, knives, jugs, straws and an espuma gun for making foams.

TERMS & TECHNIQUES

Shaking and stirring are the two most basic mixology techniques, and are essential to master to make both classic and contemporary cocktails. The other techniques described here – building, layering, muddling, blending, creating foams and airs and infusing – all add to your repertoire of bartender's techniques.

SHAKING AND STIRRING

Shaking is when you add all the ingredients, with the specified amount of ice cubes, to the shaker and shake vigorously for approximately 5–10 seconds. The benefits of shaking are that the drink is rapidly mixed, chilled and aerated. Once the drink has been shaken, the outside of the shaker should be lightly frosted.

Shaking a mocktail will dilute your drink quite significantly. This gives recipes the correct balance of taste and temperature. The drink is then double-strained into glasses – the shaker could have an inbuilt strainer and you usually use a separate strainer over the glass as well. Shaking is also used to prepare mocktails that include an ingredient that will not combine with less vigorous forms of mixing, such as egg white.

Stirring is the purist's choice, a mixing technique where you combine all the ingredients, usually with some ice cubes, in a mixing glass and stir them together using a long-handled bar spoon or swizzle stick. This allows you to blend and chill the ingredients without too much erosion of the ice, so you can control the level of dilution.

BUILDING AND LAYERING

Building involves the pouring of all the ingredients, one by one, usually over ice, into the serving glass. You might then stir the mocktail briefly to mix it rather than to chill or aerate it. You need to follow built recipes exactly, as the order of the ingredients can vary and this can affect the flavour.

Layering requires concentration, precision and a steady hand. To make layered mocktails, you generally pour the heaviest liquid first, working through to the lightest. However, the real trick is the technique. Either touch the top of the drink with a long-handled bar spoon and pour the liquid slowly over the back of it to disperse it across the top of the ingredients already in the glass, or pour the liquid down the twisted stem that many bar spoons have. You should hold the spoon's flat disc just above the drink. Use a clean bar spoon for each layer. Floating is the term used to describe adding the top layer.

MUDDLING AND BLENDING

Muddling is the extraction of the juice or oils from the pulp or skin of a fruit, herb or spice. It involves mashing ingredients to release their flavours and it is usually done with a large pestle-like implement called a muddler.

The end of the muddler that is used to crush ingredients is thicker, flatter and sometimes spiked. The best muddling technique is to keep pressing down with a twisting action until the ingredient has released all its oil or juice. You can also use a pestle and mortar or the end of a wooden spoon.

Blending is when all mocktail ingredients are combined in a blender or food processor. This is used when mixing ingredients such as whole fruit, or with creamy ingredients that do not combine well unless they are blended.

These drinks are often blended with crushed or cracked ice to produce mocktails with a smooth, frozen consistency.

FOAMS AND AIRS

Foams and airs can be created in various thicknesses, from a light froth to a heavy, creamy foam. For a simple foam, use egg white, lemon juice and sugar – to top two mocktails, just whisk 1 egg white, ½ measure of lemon juice and 1 teaspoon of caster sugar together until thoroughly mixed. This mixture can then be placed into an espuma gun or cream whipper, charged, shaken and sprayed over the top of the mocktails for a light, creamy finish. The fresher the egg white, the more stable the foam.

An air is an extremely light froth with an effervescent texture that is less heavy than a foam – the texture can range from a bubble bath foam to a light fizz. To make a light air, the best ingredient to use is lecithin. Whisk a pinch of powdered lecithin with sugar syrup using a hand whisk or electric mixer until you have a light air. If you prefer a finer air, use a milk frother.

INFUSIONS

Infusions allow you to combine flavours to produce some inventive new ingredients. When you make a cup of tea, the tea leaves change the colour and taste of the water they have infused. It is the same with mixed drinks. You can infuse water, syrups, juices and even condiments. To infuse flavours, you need to steep them in your choice of ingredient for a minimum of 24 hours. When the right strength of flavour has imparted, the solids are strained out. The infused ingredient can then be stored in the fridge for up to 2 weeks.

Creating infusions means that you will always have flavoured mixtures to hand, instead of having to muddle ingredients each time. The depth of flavour should be strong, depending on how long the infusions have been left to mix.

CHAPTER

<<< 1 >>>

FRESH

These mocktails immerse themselves in nature's bounty and in the cool and refreshing – here we embrace apples, pears, mint, rosewater, clean tastes, crisp produce, pure ingredients and hydrating, uplifting combinations.

LAVENDER LEMONADE

INGREDIENTS

250 ml/9 fl oz boiling water
10 g/¼ oz lavender heads
75 g/2¾ oz sugar
ice cubes
60 ml/2 fl oz fresh lemon juice
150 ml/5 fl oz chilled sparkling water
lavender sprig, to decorate
lemon wheel, to decorate, if you like

1. Put the boiling water into a small pan or heatproof bowl and add the lavender heads. Then add the sugar and stir to dissolve.

2. Cover and leave in the refrigerator overnight to infuse.

3. Strain into a clean bottle and store in the refrigerator.

4. Fill a highball glass with ice cubes and add 50 ml/2 fl oz of the lavender syrup. Add the lemon juice and stir to mix.

5. Top with sparkling water, decorate with a lavender sprig and lemon wheel and serve immediately.

APPLE MINT CHILL

INGREDIENTS

ice cubes

4 tsp elderflower cordial

2 tbsp fresh lemon juice

125 ml/4 fl oz cloudy apple juice

6 fresh mint leaves

3½ tbsp soda water

fresh mint sprig, to decorate

apple fan, to decorate

---

1. Fill a highball glass with ice cubes and add the cordial, lemon juice and apple juice. Stir well to mix.

2. Bruise the mint, add to the glass and stir again.

3. Top with soda water, garnish with the mint sprig and an apple fan and serve immediately.

VANILLA ICED TEA

<<< SERVES 1 >>>

INGREDIENTS

2 tsp fresh lemon juice

3 fresh mint leaves

ice cubes

125 ml/4 fl oz cold breakfast tea
or peppermint tea

fresh mint sprig, to decorate

lemon wheel, to decorate

VANILLA SYRUP

1 split vanilla pod

bottle agave syrup

---

1. Add the split vanilla pod to the bottle of agave syrup
and leave it in the bottle to infuse. The pod can
stay in the bottle as you use the infused agave.

2. Put the lemon juice and 2 tsp of the syrup into
the base of a rocks glass and stir to dissolve the agave.

3. Crush the mint leaves and add to the glass.

4. Fill the glass with ice cubes and pour over the tea.

5. Stir well to mix and garnish with a mint sprig and lemon wheel.

SHIRLEY TEMPLE

INGREDIENTS

cracked ice cubes
2 measures lemon juice
½ measure grenadine
½ measure sugar syrup
ginger ale
orange slice, to decorate

1. Put 4–6 cracked ice cubes into a cocktail shaker.

2. Pour over the lemon juice, grenadine and sugar syrup and shake vigorously until well frosted.

3. Half-fill a chilled highball glass with cracked ice, then strain the cocktail over it.

4. Top up with ginger ale and decorate with the orange slice. Serve immediately.

PROHIBITION PUNCH

INGREDIENTS

850 ml/1½ pints apple juice
350 ml/12 fl oz lemon juice
125 ml/4 fl oz sugar syrup
cracked ice cubes
2¼ litres/4 pints ginger ale
orange slices, to decorate

---

1. Pour the apple juice into a large jug.

2. Add the lemon juice and sugar syrup
and a handful of cracked ice cubes.

3. Add the ginger ale and stir gently to mix.

4. Pour into chilled lowball glasses and decorate
with the orange slices. Serve immediately.

LONG BOAT

‹‹‹ **SERVES 1** ›››

INGREDIENTS

ice cubes
1 measure lime cordial
ginger beer
lime wedge, to decorate
fresh mint sprig, to decorate

---

1. Fill a chilled glass two-thirds full with the ice and pour in the lime cordial.

2. Top up with ginger beer and stir gently.

3. Decorate with the lime wedge and the mint sprig. Serve immediately.

HEALTH ‹‹‹ BENEFITS ››› OF MOCKTAILS

Drinking mocktails has significant advantages over drinking alcohol. To begin with, any type of alcohol comes at a price, so because mocktails remove the alcohol, the final mocktails are less expensive.

Alcoholic drinks, sugary mixed drinks or fruit concoctions can add copious calories to your daily allowance. The average mixed drink with a single shot of spirit with high sugar content, juice or flavoured soda totals around 200 calories. Times that by two or three over the course of an evening and you will have to run an extra hour to burn it off. Mocktails made with fresh fruit, sensible syrups and edible garnishes can come in at around half or less of this calorie value.

Mocktails also generally have more nutrients than cocktails. Those made with fresh and/or organic juices, such as pomegranate, mango and cranberry, boast plenty of antioxidants and vitamin C. Drinks containing these ingredients also mean that you will be consuming natural sugars.

Finally, mocktails can be enjoyed by everyone – designated drivers, pregnant women, people on medication or with chronic illnesses, children and the most devout teetotallers. This makes for a more inclusive atmosphere at a party or other event where everyone has an interesting choice of drinks.

POMEGRANATE & ROSE SHERBET

◄ INGREDIENTS ►

crushed ice, to serve

8 fresh mint sprigs, to decorate
(optional)

sparkling or still water, to serve

POMEGRANATE & ROSE SYRUP

juice of 2 lemons

¼ tsp rosewater

200 ml/7 fl oz fresh pomegranate juice
(juice of about 2 pomegranates)

200 g/7 oz caster sugar

1. To make the syrup, put the lemon juice, rosewater, pomegranate juice and sugar in a saucepan, stir and cook over a low heat until the sugar has dissolved.

2. Increase the heat to medium–high, bring to the boil, then reduce the heat to low and simmer for 3–4 minutes. Boiling sugar is very hot, so handle with care and make sure it doesn't bubble over. Leave to cool completely.

3. Put some crushed ice in a tall glass. Pour a dash of the syrup over the ice and add a sprig of mint, if using. Pour in still or sparkling water to taste, mix well and serve immediately.

4. The syrup will keep in the refrigerator in a sealed container for 3–4 days.

ITALIAN SODA

INGREDIENTS

cracked ice cubes
1½ measures hazelnut syrup
sparkling water
lime slice, to decorate

---

1. Fill a chilled Collins glass with cracked ice.

2. Pour the hazelnut syrup over and fill with sparkling water. Stir gently and dress with a slice of lime. Serve immediately.

ARNOLD
PALMER

<<< SERVES 1 >>>

INGREDIENTS

ice cubes
3 measures lemonade
3 measures iced tea

---

1. Half fill a chilled highball glass
with ice cubes and pour in the lemonade.

2. Slowly pour in the tea, so that it does not mix.

3. Serve immediately with a straw.

VIRGIN
GINGER FIZZ

‹‹‹ SERVES 1 ›››

INGREDIENTS

ginger ale
3 fresh mint sprigs
cracked ice cubes
fresh raspberries, to decorate
fresh mint sprig, to decorate

1. Put 2 measures of ginger ale into a blender.

2. Add the mint sprigs and blend together.

3. Strain into a chilled highball glass that is two-thirds filled with cracked ice. Top up with more ginger ale.

4. Decorate with raspberries and the mint sprig. Serve immediately.

VIRGIN
BITTER GUNNER

<<< **SERVES 1** >>>

INGREDIENTS

4–6 ice cubes

50 ml/2 fl oz lime juice

2 tsp Angostura bitters,
or to taste

200 ml/7 fl oz ginger beer

200 ml/7 fl oz lemonade

lime slice, to decorate

1. Mix all the ingredients together
in a highball glass.

2. Taste and add more angostura bitters if you wish.

3. Add the lime slice to the glass
and serve immediately.

SALTY PUPPY

INGREDIENTS

granulated sugar
coarse salt
wedge of lime
cracked ice cubes
½ measure lime juice
grapefruit juice

1. Mix equal quantities of the sugar and salt together on a saucer.

2. Rub the rim of a chilled highball glass with a wedge of lime and dip it into the sugar and salt mixture to frost.

3. Fill the glass with cracked ice and pour the lime juice over them. Top up with grapefruit juice and serve immediately.

VIRGIN COLLINS

<<< **SERVES 1** >>>

INGREDIENTS

6 fresh mint leaves,
plus extra to decorate

1 tsp caster sugar

2 measures lemon juice

cracked ice cubes

sparkling water

lemon slice, to decorate

---

1. Put the mint leaves into a chilled Collins or highball glass.

2. Add the sugar and lemon juice.

3. Crush the mint leaves, then stir until the sugar has dissolved.

4. Fill the glass with cracked ice cubes and top up with sparkling water. Stir gently and decorate with the fresh mint and lemon slice. Serve immediately.

ORANGE & LIME FIZZ

<<< **SERVES 1** >>>

2 measures chilled fresh orange juice
icing sugar
squeeze lime juice
few drops Angostura bitters
2–3 measures chilled sparkling water

---

1. Rub the rim of a flute with orange or lime juice
and dip into the icing sugar.

2. Stir the rest of the juices together with the bitters
and then pour into the glass.

3. Add sparkling water to taste and serve immediately.

GRAPEFRUIT COOLER

◀ **INGREDIENTS** ▶

55 g/2 oz fresh mint
2 measures sugar syrup
475 ml/16 fl oz grapefruit juice
4 measures lemon juice
cracked ice cubes
sparkling mineral water
fresh mint sprigs, to decorate

1. Muddle fresh mint leaves in a small bowl with the sugar syrup.

2. Set aside for at least 2 hours to steep, mashing again from time to time.

3. Strain the steeped mixture into a pitcher and add the grapefruit juice and lemon juice. Cover with cling film and chill for at least 2 hours, until required.

4. To serve, fill six chilled Collins glasses with cracked ice. Divide the cocktail among the glasses and fill with sparkling water. Dress with fresh mint and serve immediately.

HONEYDEW COOLER

INGREDIENTS

250 g/9 oz honeydew
melon

300 ml/10 fl oz sparkling
mineral water

2 tbsp clear honey

1. Cut the rind off the melon. Chop the melon into
chunks, discarding any seeds.

2. Put into a food processor with the water and
honey and process until smooth. Pour into glasses
and serve immediately.

APPLE
FRAZZLE

<<< **SERVES 1** >>>

INGREDIENTS

4 measures apple juice

1 tsp sugar syrup

½ tsp lemon juice

ice cubes

sparkling mineral water

apple slice, to decorate

---

1. Shake the apple juice, sugar syrup and lemon juice vigorously over ice until well frosted.

2. Strain into a chilled tumbler and top up with sparkling mineral water. Dress with a slice of apple and serve immediately.

PINEAPPLE
& MINT ICED TEA

<<< **SERVES 4** >>>

1 pineapple

1 litre/1¾ pints water

30 g/1 oz fresh mint sprigs

5-cm/2-inch piece of fresh ginger,
finely sliced

125 ml/4 fl oz agave syrup

crushed ice

2 tbsp fresh mint leaves, to decorate

1. Prepare the pineapple by slicing off the base and leaves with a sharp knife. Rest the pineapple on its base and slice off the peel, until you reveal the flesh. Slice the fruit in half and remove the woody core that sits down the centre. Cut the remaining flesh into 2-cm/¾-inch cubes.

2. Pour the water into a large saucepan and add the pineapple, mint and ginger. Stir in the agave syrup and place the saucepan over a medium–high heat. Simmer for 45 minutes, or until the liquid has reduced by half.

3. Remove from the heat and allow the nectar to cool completely and infuse. This will take 4–5 hours. Using a slotted spoon, remove the mint sprigs and ginger.

4. Empty the crushed ice into the bottom of a large jug and add the fresh mint leaves. Pour over the cooled nectar and stir to mix. Serve immediately.

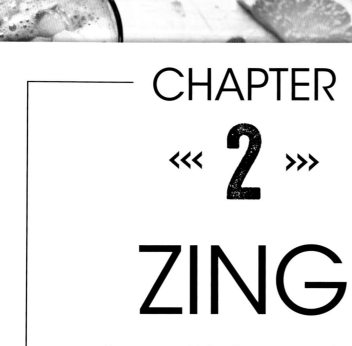

CHAPTER

««« 2 »»»

ZING

Here are mocktails with a penchant for citrus
flavours and reviving combinations – discover
the tang of lemon, orange, grapefruit and lime,
and the clean-cut tastes of pomegranate, grape
and ginger, finished with citrus peel curls, orange
slices and wedges of lime.

QUEEN OF GREENS

INGREDIENTS

4 kale leaves, stems included
ice cubes
6 fresh mint leaves
4 tsp ginger syrup
2 tbsp fresh lime juice
fresh mint sprig, to decorate

1. Juice the kale leaves using a juicer.

2. Fill a cocktail shaker with ice cubes, add the kale juice, the mint leaves, the ginger syrup and the lime juice, and shake hard for 15 seconds.

3. Put 4–5 ice cubes into a large wine glass and strain the mocktail over it.

4. Decorate with the mint sprig and serve immediately.

SAINT KIDD

INGREDIENTS

ice cubes

2 tsp apple pie syrup

1 tbsp fresh lime juice

100 ml/3½ fl oz apple juice

50 ml/2 fl oz spicy ginger beer

lime wedge, to decorate

---

1. Fill a highball glass with ice cubes and add the syrup.

2. Add the lime juice and apple juice, stir well and top up with the ginger beer.

3. Decorate with the lime wedge and serve immediately.

PINK
FIZZ

<<< **SERVES 1** >>>

INGREDIENTS

5 tsp chilled pomegranate juice

125 ml/4 fl oz chilled ginger ale

1 tsp pomegranate seeds,
to decorate

---

1. Pour the pomegranate juice into a
champagne flute.

2. Top with chilled ginger ale.

3. Decorate with the pomegranate seeds
and serve immediately.

LEMON FIZZ

INGREDIENTS

2 fresh lemons
crushed ice
peel of ½ lemon
1 tbsp sugar
iced lemonade

1. Squeeze the fresh lemons and pour the juice into a chilled highball glass filled with crushed ice.

2. Add the lemon peel and sugar to taste and stir briefly.

3. Top up with lemonade to taste and serve immediately.

ST CLEMENTS

‹‹‹ SERVES 2 ›››

INGREDIENTS

ice cubes

2 measures orange juice

2 measures bitter lemon

orange and lemon slices,
to decorate

1. Put the ice cubes into a chilled tumbler.
Pour in the orange juice and bitter lemon.

2. Stir gently and dress with the slices
of orange and lemon. Serve immediately.

FRESH
‹‹‹ IS ›››
BEST

Many mocktail recipes call for 'fresh' juices, but what does this really mean? And why are fresh juices better than cartons of juice from a store? Essentially, a fresh juice is one that is juiced or squeezed directly from the fruit without any processing. Using freshly squeezed fruit juices has significant benefits, both to the flavour of your mocktails and to your physical health. Fresh homemade juices contain more vitamins, minerals and nutritional compounds such as enzymes and flavonoids than commercial juices, which will lose their goodness over time and may contain added sugar.

Fresh fruit and vegetable juices can also assist with digestion. This is because a liquid is easier to digest than solids, so your digestive system doesn't have to work so hard. The soluble fibre in fresh juices can also help to lower cholesterol. Fresh juice also plays a part in flushing out built-up toxins in the body.

Although you might think that squeezing fresh juice is a time-consuming job, drinking it can in fact help you preserve your energy stores. Our bodies use energy to convert the foods we eat into a liquid state ready to be absorbed, so when you drink fresh juice, your body essentially skips this step and saves energy. This is the reason that your body feels revived after a healthy meal and at a low ebb after eating junk food.

NON-ALCOHOLIC PIMM'S

INGREDIENTS

600 ml/1 pint chilled lemonade
450 ml/15 fl oz chilled cola
450 ml/15 fl oz chilled dry ginger ale
juice of 1 orange
juice of 1 lemon
few drops Angostura bitters
sliced fruit
fresh mint sprigs
ice cubes

1. Mix the first six ingredients together thoroughly in a large jug or punch bowl.

2. Float in the fruit and mint. Keep the Pimm's in a cold place and add the ice cubes just before serving.

POM POM

INGREDIENTS

juice of ½ lemon
1 egg white
1 dash grenadine
ice cubes
lemonade
lemon slice, to decorate

1. Shake the lemon juice, egg white and grenadine together and strain over the ice cubes in a tall glass.

2. Top up with lemonade and dress with a lemon slice on the rim of the glass. Serve immediately.

PINKY PINK

INGREDIENTS

1 measure lemon juice

1 measure orange juice

2–3 strawberries, mashed

1 measure strawberry syrup

½ egg yolk

1 dash grenadine

ice cubes

strawberry slice, to decorate

---

1. Place the lemon juice, orange juice, strawberries, strawberry syrup, egg yolk and grenadine in a cocktail shaker and add ice cubes. Shake vigorously.

2. Strain the mixture into a cocktail glass and decorate with the strawberry slice. Serve immediately.

MAIDENLY MIMOSA

‹‹‹ SERVES 2 ›››

INGREDIENTS

175 ml/6 fl oz orange juice

175 ml/6 fl oz sparkling white grape juice

orange slices, to decorate

1. Chill two champagne flutes.

2. Divide the orange juice between the flutes and top up with the sparkling grape juice.

3. Decorate with the orange slices and serve immediately.

SLUSH PUPPY

<<< **SERVES 1** >>>

INGREDIENTS

juice of 1 lemon or ½ pink grapefruit

30 ml/1 fl oz grenadine

ice cubes

few strips of lemon peel

2–3 tsp raspberry syrup

soda water

cherry, to decorate

---

1. Pour the lemon juice and grenadine into a chilled tall glass with ice.

2. Add the lemon peel, syrup and soda water to taste. Decorate with a cherry and serve immediately.

LITTLE PRINCE

INGREDIENTS

cracked ice cubes

1 measure apricot juice

1 measure lemon juice

2 measures sparkling
apple juice

lemon peel twist, to decorate

1. Put the cracked ice into a mixing glass. Pour the apricot juice, lemon juice and apple juice over the ice and stir well.

2. Strain into a chilled highball glass and dress with a lemon twist. Serve immediately.

BLOOD ON THE TRACKS

INGREDIENTS

½ measure Campari bitters

ice cubes

2½ measures blood orange juice

sparkling water

orange slice, to decorate

fresh mint sprig, to decorate

---

1. Pour the bitters into a chilled highball glass filled with ice.

2. Add the blood orange juice. Do not stir.

3. Top up with sparkling water.

4. Decorate with the orange slice and mint and serve immediately.

PARSON'S PARTICULAR

INGREDIENTS

2 measures fresh orange juice

1 measure fresh lemon juice

1 egg yolk

4 dashes grenadine

cracked ice cubes

cocktail cherry, to decorate

---

1. Shake all the ingredients together over ice until well frosted and strain into a long glass.

2. Dress with a cocktail cherry. Serve immediately.

APPLE SOUR

<<< SERVES 1 >>>

INGREDIENTS

4 measures apple juice
juice of 1 lemon
juice of 1 lime
1 measure clear honey
1 small egg white
crushed ice
4–5 raspberries
long apple peel strip, to decorate

---

1. Blend the apple juice, lemon and lime juice, honey, egg white and ice in a blender until frothy and partly frozen.

2. Put the raspberries in the bottom of an iced tall glass, crush with a wooden spoon, and pour in the fruit slush.

3. Dress with a strip of apple peel. Serve immediately.

RED APPLE SUNSET

INGREDIENTS

2 measures apple juice
2 measures grapefruit juice
1 dash grenadine
ice cubes

1. Shake the apple juice, grapefruit juice and a dash of grenadine over ice cubes until well frosted.

2. Strain into a chilled cocktail glass and serve immediately.

SOBER SUNDAY

INGREDIENTS

50 ml/2 fl oz grenadine

50 ml/2 fl oz fresh lemon
or lime juice

ice cubes

lemonade

fresh lemon or lime slices,
to decorate

1. Pour the grenadine and fruit juice into an ice
filled highball glass.

2. Top up with lemonade and finish with slices of
lemon or lime. Serve immediately.

DUSTY SUNRISE

INGREDIENTS

cracked ice cubes
2 measures orange juice
1 measure lemon juice
1 measure grenadine
sparkling mineral water

1. Put the cracked ice into a chilled highball glass and pour the orange juice, lemon juice and grenadine over it.

2. Stir together well and top up with sparkling mineral water. Serve immediately.

JUICY JULEP

INGREDIENTS

1 measure orange juice
1 measure pineapple juice
1 measure lime juice
½ measure raspberry syrup
4 crushed fresh mint leaves
cracked ice cubes
ginger ale
fresh mint sprig, to decorate

1. Shake the first five ingredients vigorously over ice until well frosted.

2. Strain into a chilled Collins glass, top up with ginger ale and stir gently. Dress with mint.

SOFT SANGRIA

<<< **SERVES 10** >>>

INGREDIENTS

1.5 litres/2½ pints chilled red grape juice
300 ml/10 fl oz chilled orange juice
75 ml/2½ fl oz chilled cranberry juice
50 ml/2 fl oz lemon juice
50 ml/2 fl oz lime juice
100 ml/3½ fl oz sugar syrup
ice cubes
lemon, orange and lime slices,
to decorate

1. Put the grape juice, orange juice, cranberry juice, lemon juice, lime juice and sugar syrup into a chilled punch bowl and stir well.

2. Add the ice and decorate with the slices of lemon, orange and lime. Serve immediately.

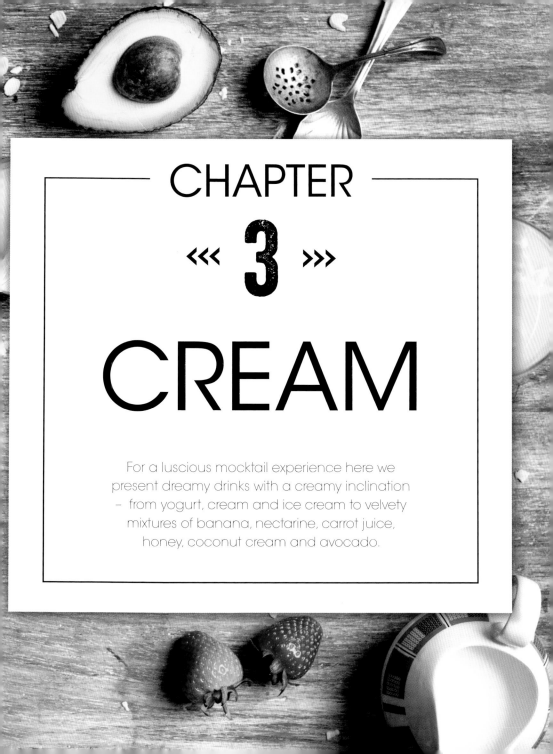

CHAPTER

««« 3 »»»

CREAM

For a luscious mocktail experience here we present dreamy drinks with a creamy inclination – from yogurt, cream and ice cream to velvety mixtures of banana, nectarine, carrot juice, honey, coconut cream and avocado.

AVOCADO THYME

INGREDIENTS

½ large avocado
pinch of salt
4–6 ice cubes
2½ tbsp fresh lime juice
2 tsp agave syrup
3 fresh thyme sprigs
60 ml/2 fl oz soda water

---

1. Muddle the avocado with the salt in a cocktail shaker.

2. Add the ice cubes, lime juice, agave syrup and 2 thyme sprigs and shake hard.

3. Double strain into a hurricane glass and top with the soda water.

4. Decorate with a fresh thyme sprig and serve immediately.

PEANUT CUP

<<< SERVES 1 >>>

INGREDIENTS

ice cubes
2 tbsp puréed banana
2 tsp peanut butter powder
150 ml/5 fl oz skimmed milk
banana slices, to decorate

1. Put all the ingredients into a cocktail shaker filled with ice cubes.

2. Shake hard and pour directly from the shaker into a highball glass.

3. Decorate with banana slices and serve immediately.

THE MOCKTAIL
≪ GARNISH ≫

Whether a bright piece of fruit, a briny olive or a festive umbrella, the garnish has a solid place in the history of mixed drinks. In the case of fruit wedges, slices or twists, the garnish imbues a flavour of juice or citrus oil to the drink. Likewise, an olive or onion lends a whisper of savoury flavour. There are also bright red cherries, adding sweetness and colour to drinks.

When cutting citrus wedges and slices, top and tail the fruit ends and cut the fruit in half lengthwise. For wedges, cut each side in half, and in half again, giving you eight wedges per fruit. For slices, slice each half to a width of 5mm/¼ inch. To create a citrus peel, use a vegetable peeler, fruit knife or canelle knife. Start by cutting the bottom off the fruit and cut away from you. Remove the pith before using.

Flamed orange is a dramatic garnish that will impart a burnt orange flavour to drinks. To do this, cut a thick piece of peel, hold it lengthwise between your thumb and forefinger and using a lighter, gently burn the outer skin of the peel to draw out the oils. Then squeeze the orange peel inwards to express the oils through the flame. Care should be taken when attempting this technique.

Garnish skewers can be made from bamboo, wood, plastic or even rosemary sprigs. Generally used for softer fruits such as berries, skewers can also create more intricate garnishes such as an apple fan. Sprigs of herbs are another garnish idea – these reflect the ingredients in the mocktail and endow the drink with a deeper aroma. Herb sprigs also have great natural panache!

ALMONDINE

INGREDIENTS

2 measures peach juice
4 measures cold milk
few drops almond extract
1–2 tbsp clover honey
1 small egg
ice cubes
toasted almonds, to decorate

1. Shake the first six ingredients together well until frosted.

2. Pour into a large cocktail glass or wine glass and sprinkle the almonds on top.

CARROT CREAM

INGREDIENTS

2 measures carrot juice
2½ measures single cream
1 measure orange juice
cracked ice cubes
1 egg yolk
orange slice, to decorate

---

1. Pour the carrot juice, cream and orange juice over ice in a shaker and add the egg yolk. Shake vigorously until well mixed.

2. Strain into a chilled glass and dress with the slice of orange. Serve immediately.

MANGO LASSI

<<< **SERVES 2** >>>

◄━━ **INGREDIENTS** ━━►

125 ml/4 fl oz plain yogurt
225 ml/8 fl oz milk
1 tbsp rose water
3 tbsp honey
1 ripe mango, peeled and diced
6 ice cubes
rose petals, to decorate

━━━━━━━

1. Pour the yogurt and milk into a food processor and process until combined. Add the rose water and honey and process until blended, then add the mango and ice cubes and blend until smooth.

2. Pour into chilled glasses. Dress with rose petals. Serve immediately.

MINI COLADA

<<< **SERVES 1** >>>

INGREDIENTS

cracked ice cubes
6 measures milk
3 measures coconut cream
4 measures pineapple juice

TO DECORATE

pineapple chunk
pineapple leaf
cocktail cherry

1. Put 4–6 cracked ice cubes into a cocktail shaker.

2. Pour over the milk and coconut cream.

3. Add the pineapple juice and shake vigorously until well frosted.

4. Half-fill a highball glass with cracked ice, strain the cocktail into it and decorate with the pineapple chunk, pineapple leaf and cherry. Serve immediately.

COCO
BERRY

<<< SERVES 1 >>>

INGREDIENTS

90 g/3¼ oz raspberries

crushed ice

1 measure coconut cream

150 ml/5 fl oz pineapple juice

pineapple wedge, to decorate

a few raspberries, to decorate

1. Rub the raspberries through a strainer with the back of a spoon and transfer the purée to a blender.

2. Add the crushed ice, coconut cream and pineapple juice and blend until smooth, then pour the mixture, without straining, into a chilled lowball glass.

3. Dress with a pineapple wedge and fresh raspberries. Serve immediately.

BABYLOVE

INGREDIENTS

300 ml/10 fl oz cold milk
12–14 strawberries, hulled
½ ripe avocado
1 measure lemon juice

---

1. Place all the ingredients except 2 strawberries in a blender and blend for 15–20 seconds, until smooth.

2. Pour into iced tall glasses and dress each one with slices of strawberry.

BEE POLLEN & NECTARINE SHAKE

<<< SERVES 2 >>>

INGREDIENTS

2 ripe nectarines, quartered
200 ml/7 fl oz semi-skimmed milk
2 tbsp Greek-style natural yogurt
1 tbsp bee pollen
1 tsp runny honey
handful of ice cubes
1 tsp bee pollen, to decorate
2 slices nectarine, to decorate

1. Place the the nectarines, milk, yogurt, bee pollen and honey in a blender and whizz until smooth. Add the ice cubes and whizz again until completely blended.

2. Pour the milkshake into chilled glasses and decorate with the bee pollen and a fresh slice of nectarine. Serve immediately.

MOCHA SLUSH

INGREDIENTS

crushed ice

100 ml/3½ fl oz coffee syrup

45 ml/1½ fl oz chocolate syrup

200 ml/7 fl oz milk

grated chocolate, to decorate

1. Whizz the crushed ice in a small blender with the coffee and chocolate syrups and milk until slushy.

2. Pour into a chilled glass and sprinkle with grated chocolate. Serve immediately.

FRUIT
COOLER

<<< **SERVES 2** >>>

INGREDIENTS

225 ml/8 fl oz orange juice
125 ml/4 fl oz natural yogurt
2 eggs
2 bananas, sliced and frozen
fresh banana slices

1. Pour the orange juice and yogurt into a food processor and process gently until combined.

2. Add the eggs and frozen bananas and process until smooth.

3. Pour the mixture into highball or hurricane glasses and decorate the rims with slices of fresh banana. Serve immediately.

APPLE PIE CREAM

<<< SERVES 1 >>>

INGREDIENTS

4–6 cracked ice cubes

4 measures apple juice

1 small scoop vanilla
ice cream

soda water

cinnamon sugar, to
decorate

apple slice, to decorate

---

1. Put the cracked ice cubes into a blender
and add the apple juice and ice cream.

2. Blend for 10–15 seconds until frothy and frosted.
Pour into a glass and top up with soda water.

3. Sprinkle over the cinnamon sugar and decorate
with an apple slice. Serve immediately.

CHAPTER
⟪⟪⟪ 4 ⟫⟫⟫
BERRY

Berries are bountiful in nature, and abundant, too, in this collection of mocktails. Presented in solo glory or in lively berry mixes, delight in them all – blackberries, juniper berries, strawberries, raspberries, grapes and cranberries.

BLACKBERRY COLLINS

INGREDIENTS

9 fresh blackberries
3 tsp blood orange juice
125 ml/4 fl oz sparkling water
blood orange slice, to decorate
LEMONADE SYRUP
4 unwaxed lemons
125 g/4½ oz sugar
150 ml/5 fl oz water

1. To make the lemonade syrup, zest the lemons and squeeze the juice into a saucepan. Add the sugar and water and place over a medium heat until the sugar has dissolved.

2. Strain the mixture and leave to cool, then pour into a clean bottle and store in the refrigerator for up to 4 weeks.

3. Muddle 8 of the blackberries in a cocktail shaker with the orange juice.

4. Strain into a highball glass and top up with the lemonade syrup and sparkling water.

5. Decorate with the remaining blackberry and a blood orange slice and serve immediately.

JUNIPER JULEP

INGREDIENTS

500 ml/17 fl oz white grape juice
8–10 juniper berries
½ tsp agave syrup
2 tsp fresh lime juice
5 fresh fresh mint leaves
crushed ice
fresh mint sprig, to decorate
2 grapes, to decorate

---

1. Pour the grape juice into a jug. Add the juniper berries, stir well, then leave to infuse for 3 hours. Strain the juice into a clean bottle and store in the refrigerator.

2. Mix the agave syrup and lime juice in a julep tin or highball glass to dissolve the syrup.

3. Bruise the mint leaves and add to the tin.

4. Fill the tin with crushed ice, then pour in 125 ml/4 fl oz of the infused grape juice. Stir (or 'churn') the mixture through the ice.

5. Top up with crushed ice, decorate with a mint sprig and two grapes and serve immediately.

STRAWBERRY MULE

INGREDIENTS

3 fresh strawberries
50 ml/2 fl oz pineapple juice
2 tsp fresh lime juice
ice cubes
100 ml/3½ fl oz ginger beer
½ strawberry, to decorate
lime wedge, to decorate

---

1. Muddle the strawberries in a copper mule mug or a highball glass.

2. Add the pineapple juice and lime and stir well to mix.

3. Add ice cubes to fill the mug. Top with the ginger beer and stir again.

4. Decorate with a strawberry half and a lime wedge and serve immediately.

SUPER BERRY HI-BALL

INGREDIENTS

4 strawberries
6 raspberries
2 tsp fresh lime juice
2 fresh basil leaves
1 tsp agave syrup
ice cubes
60 ml/2 fl oz soda water
berry skewer, to decorate

1. Muddle the strawberries, raspberries, lime juice, basil and agave syrup in a cocktail shaker.

2. Fill the shaker with ice cubes and shake hard.

3. Fill a large wine glass with ice cubes and strain the cocktail over.

4. Top with soda water and stir gently, then decorate with a berry skewer and serve immediately.

MAKING
⋘ A SYRUP ⋙

A syrup – a combination of sugar and water – will sweeten and add flavour to mocktails and cocktails. As with shrubs, there are two ways to make home-made syrups, a hot process and a cold process. Using the hot method is quicker and can give a more mellow flavour syrup, whereas one made with a cold process provides a more vibrant flavour, and generally one that is truer to the original ingredients. The following recipe is made using the cold process. This syrup works wonderfully topped with light tonic water or soda water. It can also be shaken with apple juice and fresh mint for a mocktail twist on a julep.

BASIL & LIME SYRUP
3 whole limes, peeled; 30 g/1 oz fresh basil leaves;
350 g/12 oz caster sugar; 200 ml/7 fl oz cold water

1. Muddle the lime peels, basil leaves and sugar together in a bowl. Cover the bowl in clingfilm and set aside for at least 2 hours.
2. Remove the peels from the sugar and add the water. Place the contents in a sealed container and shake hard to dissolve the sugar.
3. Pour the mixture through a fine-mesh strainer and decant into a clean, clip-top bottle. This syrup will store in the refrigerator for up to 4 weeks.

CRANBERRY PUNCH

INGREDIENTS

600 ml/1 pint cranberry juice

600 ml/1 pint orange juice

150 ml/5 fl oz water

½ tsp ground ginger

¼ tsp cinnamon

¼ tsp freshly grated nutmeg

cracked ice cubes

frozen cranberries and their leaves,
to decorate

---

1. Put the first six ingredients into a saucepan and bring to the boil. Reduce the heat and simmer for 5 minutes.

2. Remove from the heat and pour into a heatproof jug or bowl. Chill in the refrigerator.

3. Remove from the refrigerator, put cracked ice into the serving glasses, pour in the punch, and decorate with cranberries and their leaves on cocktail sticks. Serve immediately

RASPBERRY COOLER

INGREDIENTS

8 ice cubes, crushed
2 tsp raspberry syrup
475 ml/16 fl oz chilled apple juice
fresh raspberries, to decorate
apple pieces, to decorate

1. Put the ice in the glasses and pour over the raspberry syrup.

2. Fill each glass with apple juice and stir well. Dress with the raspberries and pieces of apple.

CRANBERRY ENERGIZER

<<< **SERVES 2** >>>

INGREDIENTS

300 ml/10 fl oz
cranberry juice

125 ml/4 fl oz orange juice

55 g/2 oz fresh raspberries

1 tbsp lemon juice

fresh orange slices,
to decorate

1. Pour the cranberry juice and orange juice into
a blender and blend gently until combined.

2. Add the raspberries and lemon juice
and blend until smooth.

3. Strain into glasses and dress with the slices
of orange. Serve immediately.

BERRY BERRY RED

‹‹‹ **SERVES 1** ›››

INGREDIENTS

55 g/2 oz raspberries

4 measures cranberry juice

4 measures raspberry juice

crushed ice

1 small meringue, crumbled

blackberry-flavoured sparkling water

---

1. Set aside a couple of raspberries for later. In a blender, blend the rest of the fruit with the juice and crushed ice.

2. Add the fruit slush to a chilled tall glass and fill it with the sparkling water.

3. Dress with raspberries and the crumbled meringue. Serve immediately.

FAUX KIR ROYALE

INGREDIENTS

4–6 cracked ice cubes
1½ measures raspberry syrup
chilled sparkling apple juice

1. Put the cracked ice cubes into a mixing glass.
Pour over the raspberry syrup.

2. Stir well to mix and strain into a chilled wine glass.

3. Top up with sparkling apple juice and stir.
Serve immediately.

STRAWBERRY CRUSH

<<< **SERVES 1** >>>

◄━━ **INGREDIENTS** ━━►

1 egg white
icing sugar
55 g/2 oz ripe strawberries
juice of ½ lemon
150 ml/5 fl oz chilled lemonade
crushed ice
sugar, to taste
fresh mint sprig, to decorate

─────────

1. Lightly whisk the egg white, dip the rim of the glass into it and then into the icing sugar, and leave to dry.

2. Put aside 1 strawberry, hull the rest, and blend with the lemon juice, lemonade, crushed ice and sugar for 2–3 minutes, until smooth but frothy.

3. Pour into the frosted glass and dress with mint. Serve immediately.

SPARKLING
PEACH MELBA

INGREDIENTS

55 g/2 oz raspberries, puréed
4 measures peach juice
crushed ice
sparkling water

1. Shake the raspberry purée and peach juice over crushed ice vigorously until well frosted.

2. Strain into a tall chilled tumbler, fill with sparkling water, and stir gently. Serve immediately.

VIRGIN RASPBERRY COOLERS

INGREDIENTS

2 lemons
115 g/4 oz icing sugar
115 g/4 oz raspberries
4 drops vanilla extract
cracked ice cubes
sparkling water
fresh mint sprigs, to decorate

---

1. Cut the ends off the lemons, then scoop out and chop the flesh.

2. Put the lemon flesh in a blender with the sugar, raspberries, vanilla extract and 4–6 cracked ice cubes and blend for 2–3 minutes.

3. Half-fill four highball glasses with cracked ice and strain in the lemon mixture.

4. Top up with sparkling water and decorate with the mint sprigs. Serve immediately.

MEMORY LANE

INGREDIENTS

10 blackberries
1 tbsp icing sugar
juice of ½ lemon
juice of ½ lime
crushed ice
lemonade

1. Reserve a few berries. Place the remaining fruit in a chilled tumbler with the sugar and crush until well mashed.

2. Add the fruit juices and ice and fill with the lemonade. Top with the reserved whole berries.

CRANBERRY & ORANGE CRUSH

<<< **SERVES 1** >>>

INGREDIENTS

juice of 2 blood oranges

150 ml/5 fl oz cranberry juice

2 tbsp raspberry or other fruit syrup

sugar, to taste

crushed ice

raspberries, to decorate

1. Shake the first four ingredients well together until really frothy.

2. Pour straight into a tall ice-filled glass. Dress with raspberries. Serve immediately. This is a long and refreshing drink, but it can be sharp, so taste first, then sweeten if necessary.

CHERRY ORCHARD

INGREDIENTS

1 measure apple juice

1 measure pear juice

2 measures cranberry juice

ice cubes

pink lemonade or cherryade

fresh or glacé cherries, to decorate

pineapple wedge, to decorate

---

1. Mix the fruit juices together over ice in a chilled glass.

2. Fill with lemonade to taste and dress with cherries and pineapple. Serve immediately.

CHAPTER

««« 5 »»»

TROPIC

In search of some soft-drink sunshine?
Overflowing with exotic, tropical ingredients,
these mocktails feature mango, melon, kiwi,
passion fruit, guava and pineapple, and carry
a guaranteed feel-good factor.

COCO KIWI KIWI

<<< **SERVES 1** >>>

INGREDIENTS

2 tsp pineapple juice

2 tbsp coconut water

ice cubes

100 ml/3½ fl oz ginger ale

2 kiwi wheels, to decorate

pineapple leaf, to decorate

KIWI SHRUB

15 kiwi fruit, peeled and quartered

400 g/14 oz sugar

350 ml/12 fl oz cider vinegar

1. To make the kiwi shrub, add the kiwi fruit to a bowl with the sugar and mix well. Cover and chill in the refrigerator for 1 hour.

2. Muddle the mixture, re-cover and leave in the refrigerator overnight.

3. Strain the mixture and add the vinegar, then shake well and leave in the refrigerator overnight. Strain through muslin and store in the refrigerator in a clean jar.

4. Put 2 tablespoons of the kiwi shrub into a cocktail shaker with the pineapple juice, coconut water and ice cubes.

5. Strain into a highball glass filled with ice cubes. Top with the ginger ale and gently stir.

6. Decorate with kiwi wheels and a pineapple leaf and serve immediately.

LEMON GRASS LAGERITA

<<< SERVES 1 >>>

INGREDIENTS

juice of ½ lime

1 tsp salt

¼ lemon grass stalk

2 tbsp mango juice

200 ml/7 fl oz chilled
alcohol-free lager

---

1. Dip a highball glass in the lime juice and then in the salt to give a salted rim.

2. Muddle the lemon grass with the mango juice in a shaker and strain into the glass.

3. Top with the lager and serve immediately.

MELON BELLINI

INGREDIENTS

ice cubes
2 tsp puréed watermelon
½ tsp agave syrup
2 tsp apple juice
80 ml/2¾ fl oz ginger ale
thin watermelon slice, to decorate

---

1. Fill a cocktail shaker with ice cubes, add the watermelon purée, agave syrup and apple juice and shake hard.

2. Strain into a chilled champagne flute and top with ginger ale.

3. Decorate with a watermelon slice and serve immediately.

CINDERS

<<< **SERVES 1** >>>

◄━ **INGREDIENTS** ━►

juice of ½ orange
juice of 1 lime
150 ml/5 fl oz pineapple juice
several drops Angostura bitters
ice cubes
soda water or dry ginger ale to taste
fruit slices, to decorate

———————

1. Shake the first four ingredients well
together with ice.

2. Strain into a chilled glass and fill with
soda water to taste.

3. Finish with a few more drops of bitters, dress
with slices of fruit and serve immediately.

THAI FRUIT COCKTAIL

INGREDIENTS

1 measure pineapple juice
1 measure orange juice
½ measure lime juice
1 measure passion fruit juice
2 measures guava juice
crushed ice
flower, to decorate

1. Shake all the juices together with the crushed ice.

2. Pour into a chilled long glass, dress with a flower and serve immediately.

MELON & COCONUT MOCK MOJITO

<<< SERVES 1 >>>

INGREDIENTS

20 g/¾ oz spinach

50 g/1¾ oz coconut flesh

200 ml/7 fl oz chilled water

100 g/3½ oz cantaloupe melon,
peeled, deseeded and chopped

1 tbsp chopped fresh mint

juice of ½ lime

50 g/1¾ oz mango, peeled, stoned
and chopped, plus 1 extra slice
to decorate

crushed ice, to serve, optional

---

1. Place the spinach, coconut and water
in a blender and whizz until smooth.

2. Add the melon, mint, lime juice and mango,
and blend until smooth and creamy.

3. Pour over crushed ice, if using, and serve
immediately, decorated with a mango slice.

ISLAND COOLER

INGREDIENTS

2 measures orange juice

1 measure lemon juice

1 measure pineapple juice

1 measure papaya juice

½ tsp grenadine

cracked ice cubes

sparkling water

pineapple wedges,
to decorate

maraschino cherries,
to decorate

---

1. Shake the fruit juices and grenadine vigorously over ice until well frosted.

2. Half-fill a chilled Collins glass with cracked ice and pour the cocktail over.

3. Fill with sparkling water and stir gently. Dress with pineapple wedges and maraschino cherries and serve immediately.

MAKING
⋘ A SHRUB ⋙

Shrubs provide both sweet and tart flavours and give depth to mocktails and cocktails. They can be made using a hot or a cold process. The cold process takes a little longer, but creates a purer and brighter fruit flavour. This fruit shrub, made with the cold process, is delicious topped with light tonic water, or with hot water and fresh ginger for a cold-busting beverage in the colder months.

STRAWBERRY & MIXED PEPPERCORN SHRUB

2 whole lemons, peeled; 350 g/12 oz caster sugar; 650 g/1 lb 7 oz strawberries, hulled and quartered; 35 mixed peppercorns; 200 ml/7 fl oz cider vinegar; 50 ml/1¾ fl oz balsamic vinegar

1. Muddle the lemon peels and sugar together in a bowl. Cover the bowl with clingfilm and set aside for at least an hour.
2. Remove the peels and add the strawberries and the mixed peppercorns to the sugar and stir the ingredients to combine. Cover the bowl with clingfilm again and place in the refrigerator for a couple of hours.
3. Remove the bowl from the refrigerator and muddle the berries into the sugar to press out as much juice as possible. Add the vinegar and stir again to mix well. Cover and return to the refrigerator for 2–3 days.
4. Remove from the refrigerator, muddle the mixture again and pour through a fine mesh strainer into a clean mason jar or clip-top bottle.
5. Store in the refrigerator for a week, to allow the flavours to blend; shake before using. This shrub can be stored for up to 6 months.

ORANGE & LIME ICED TEA

<<< SERVES 2 >>>

INGREDIENTS

125 ml/4 fl oz orange juice

4 tbsp lime juice

1–2 tbsp sugar

325 ml/11 fl oz chilled fresh tea

lime wedges

8 ice cubes

orange slices, to decorate

1. Add the orange juice, lime juice, and sugar to taste to the tea.

2. Take two glasses and rub the rims with a lime wedge, then dip them in sugar to frost.

3. Fill the glasses with ice and pour on the tea. Dress with slices of orange and serve immediately.

BRIGHT GREEN COOLER

<<< **SERVES 1** >>>

INGREDIENTS

cracked ice cubes

3 measures pineapple juice

2 measures lime juice

1 measure green
peppermint syrup

ginger ale

cucumber strip, to decorate

lime slice, to decorate

---

1. Put 4–6 cracked ice cubes into a cocktail shaker.

2. Pour over the pineapple juice, lime juice and
peppermint syrup and shake vigorously until well frosted.

3. Half-fill a chilled highball glass with cracked ice and
strain the cocktail over it.

4. Top up with ginger ale and decorate with the
cucumber strip and lime slice. Serve immediately.

TROPICAL
COOLER

<<< **SERVES 1** >>>

INGREDIENTS

2 measures passion fruit juice
2 measures guava juice
2 measures orange juice
1 measure coconut milk
1–2 tsp ginger syrup
ice cubes
slice of papaya, to decorate

1. Shake all the fruit juices with the coconut milk and ginger syrup vigorously over ice until well frosted.

2. Strain into a chilled highball glass or tall wine glass and dress the rim with a thin slice of papaya. Serve immediately.

ROSE
SUNSET

<<< **SERVES 1** >>>

INGREDIENTS

125 ml/4 fl oz plain yogurt

475 ml/16 fl oz milk

1 tbsp rose water

3 tbsp honey

1 ripe mango, peeled, pitted, and diced

6 ice cubes

edible rose petals, to decorate

---

1. Process the yogurt and milk gently in a food processor until combined.

2. Add the rose water and honey, process until thoroughly blended, then add the mango and ice cubes and process until smooth.

3. Pour into glasses and dress with rose petals. Serve immediately.

HEAVENLY DAYS

<<< SERVES 1 >>>

INGREDIENTS

2 measures hazelnut syrup

2 measures lemon juice

1 tsp grenadine

cracked ice cubes

sparkling water

slice of papaya, to decorate

1. Shake the syrup, lemon juice and grenadine vigorously over ice until well frosted.

2. Half-fill a tumbler with cracked ice and strain the cocktail over them.

3. Top up with sparkling water. Stir gently and dress with a slice of papaya. Serve immediately.

BABY BELLINI

‹‹‹ SERVES 1 ›››

INGREDIENTS

2 measures peach juice
1 measure lemon juice
sparkling apple juice

1. Pour the peach juice and lemon juice
into a chilled champagne flute and stir well.

2. Top up with sparkling apple juice
and stir again. Serve immediately.

EYE OF THE HURRICANE

<<< **SERVES 1** >>>

INGREDIENTS

2 measures passion fruit syrup

1 measure lime juice

cracked ice cubes

bitter lemon

lemon slice, to decorate

---

1. Pour the passion fruit syrup and lime juice over cracked ice in a mixing glass.

2. Stir well to mix and strain into a chilled tumbler.

3. Top up with bitter lemon and dress with a slice of lemon. Serve immediately.

CHAPTER

‹‹‹ 6 ›››

KICK

Fancy some mixology spirit without the spirits?
These mocktails have dynamic ingredients that
make a bold mark – charred chillies, beetroot,
espresso, matcha green tea, turmeric, hot
pepper sauce, clam juice and cayenne pepper.

BURNT ORANGE SOURS

◄ INGREDIENTS ►

6–8 padrón peppers
500 ml/17 fl oz carrot juice
ice cubes
2 tsp fresh lemon juice
4 tbsp fresh orange juice
charred chilli, to decorate
orange twist, to decorate

———————

1. Use a chef's blowtorch to char the skins of the peppers.

2. Put the carrot juice in a jug. Leaving the charred skins on, add the peppers to the carrot juice, agitate or stir the contents and leave to infuse for 1 hour.

3. Strain, pour into a clean bottle and store in the refrigerator.

4. Fill a rocks glass with ice cubes. Pour over 100 ml/3½ fl oz of the infused carrot juice, the lemon juice and orange juice and stir.

5. Decorate with a charred pepper and an orange twist. Serve immediately.

MATCHA COLLINS

<<< SERVES 1 >>>

INGREDIENTS

2 slices fresh ginger

2 tbsp fresh lemon juice

1 tsp clear honey

large pinch of matcha green
tea powder

4–5 ice cubes

125 ml/4 fl oz ginger ale

lemon twist, to decorate

1. Muddle the ginger with the lemon and honey in a teacup.
Add the tea and stir well.

2. Add the ice cubes and slowly pour over the ginger ale.

3. Decorate with a lemon twist and serve immediately.

SMOKED MARY

<<< **SERVES 1** >>>

INGREDIENTS

ice cubes

80 ml/2¾ fl oz cold
lapsang souchong tea

100 ml/3½ fl oz tomato juice

2 tsp fresh lemon juice

3 dashes Worcestershire sauce

2 dashes hot pepper sauce

pinch of pepper

pinch of Himalayan pink salt

lemon wheel, to decorate

halved cherry tomato, to decorate

---

1. Pour all ingredients into a tall glass filled with ice cubes.

2. Stir well, decorate with a lemon wheel
and a cherry tomato, and serve immediately.

TURBO TONIC

<<< **SERVES 1** >>>

 **INGREDIENTS**

ice cubes
200 ml/7 fl oz tonic water
2 tbsp hot or chilled espresso

JUNIPER SYRUP

10–15 juniper berries
250 ml/8½ fl oz water
50 g/1¾ oz sugar

---

1. To make the juniper syrup, add the juniper berries to a saucepan with the water and sugar and bring to the boil.

2. Remove from the heat and leave to cool, then strain into a clean bottle and store in the refrigerator.

3. Fill a highball glass with ice cubes. Add 2 teaspoons of the juniper syrup, pour over the tonic water and gently stir.

4. Place a spoon against the inside edge of the glass and slowly pour the espresso over the back of the spoon to float. Serve immediately.

TURMERIC & TONIC

INGREDIENTS

4 ice cubes
¼ tsp ground turmeric
200 ml/7 fl oz tonic water
2 tsp fresh lemon juice
2 lemon wheels, to decorate

---

1. Add the ice cubes and turmeric to a highball glass.

2. Pour over the tonic water and lemon juice and stir well.

3. Decorate with the lemon wheels and serve immediately.

VIRGIN MARY

<<< SERVES 1 >>>

INGREDIENTS

4–6 cracked ice cubes
3 measures tomato juice
1 measure lemon juice
2 dashes Worcestershire sauce
1 dash hot pepper sauce
pinch of celery salt
pepper
lemon wedge, to decorate, if liked
celery stick, to decorate

1. Put the cracked ice cubes into a cocktail shaker. Pour over the tomato juice and add the lemon juice.

2. Pour in the Worcestershire sauce and hot pepper sauce. Shake vigorously until well frosted.

3. Season to taste with the celery salt and pepper, strain into a chilled glass and decorate with the lemon wedge and celery stick. Serve immediately.

PRAIRIE OYSTER

<<< SERVES 1 >>>

1 measure Worcestershire sauce
1 measure vinegar
1 measure ketchup
1 egg yolk
cayenne pepper

---

1. Pour the Worcestershire sauce, vinegar and ketchup into a chilled glass and stir to mix.

2. Add the egg yolk carefully without breaking. Do not stir, sprinkle with cayenne pepper, and down in one!

BEETROOT VIRGIN MARY

<<< SERVES 1 >>>

INGREDIENTS

30 g/1 oz raw beetroot, peeled
175 ml/6 fl oz tomato juice
1 tsp Worcestershire sauce
¼ tsp celery salt
¼ tsp pepper
1 tsp freshly grated horseradish
½ tsp hot pepper sauce
ice cubes
1 lemon slice, to decorate
celery stick, to decorate

---

1. Cut the beetroot into small pieces. Place in a cocktail shaker and crush thoroughly with a muddler or pestle to release the colour and flavour.

2. Add the tomato juice, Worcestershire sauce, celery salt, pepper, horseradish and hot pepper sauce. Stir well with a bar spoon.

3. Pour the mixture into a Collins or highball glass. Add some ice cubes and stir again.

4. Decorate the drink with the lemon slice and celery stick. Serve immediately.

CARROT CHILL

<<< **SERVES 1** >>>

INGREDIENTS

475 ml/16 fl oz carrot juice
25 g/1 oz watercress
1 tbsp lemon juice
fresh watercress sprigs, to decorate

---

1. Pour the carrot juice into a blender. Add the watercress and lemon juice and process until smooth.

2. Transfer to a jug, cover with clingfilm, and chill in the refrigerator for at least 1 hour.

3. Pour into glasses and dress with watercress. Serve immediately.

ICE
‹‹‹ TECHNIQUES ›››

Ice is a key ingredient in any mixed drink. Here are some of the ways that ice can be used in your mocktail. Crushed ice is generally used for frozen drinks or a julep. You can crush ice at home in a blender, although the heat from the motor can melt it quickly. Another way is to wrap cubed ice in a bag or tea towel and whack it with a mallet or rolling pin.

Flavoured Ice cubes can be made by filling your ice-cube tray with the juice required for your mocktail. Place the filled tray in the coldest part of your freezer and leave it for at least a day – you want the cubes to be rock solid and glacially cold. These cubes mean that your mocktail will change flavour as the ice cubes melt over time.

Garnish ice is a relatively new style of ice that enhances the flavour and appearance of a mixed drink. When filling your ice-cube tray, simply place a solid form into the tray before freezing. Make this something related to your mocktail, such as a berry, orange peel, rosemary or a chilli slice.

Ice balls are the latest craze in mixology and they can enhance the visual appeal of your mocktail creations. Silicone ice-ball makers are widely available, but you can also use a balloon to make teardrop-shaped balls. To do this, fill round balloons with around 90 ml/2 fl oz water or juice. Tie the balloon and hang them upside down in your freezer so that it does not touch anything underneath. After a day or two, cut the balloon and free your frozen ice ball.

GINGER CRUSH

INGREDIENTS

225 ml/8 fl oz carrot juice

4 tomatoes, peeled, seeded and
roughly chopped

1 tbsp lemon juice

25 g/1 oz fresh parsley

1 tbsp grated fresh ginger

6 ice cubes

125 ml/4 fl oz water

chopped parsley, to decorate

---

1. Put the carrot juice, tomatoes and lemon juice into a
food processor and process gently until combined. Add the
parsley, ginger and ice cubes. Process until well combined,
pour in the water, and process until smooth.

2. Pour the mixture into tall glasses and dress with the
chopped parsley. Serve immediately.

BITE OF THE APPLE

INGREDIENTS

crushed ice

5 measures apple juice

1 measure lime juice

½ tsp orgeat syrup

1 tbsp apple sauce
or apple purée

ground cinnamon

1. Whizz the crushed ice in a blender with the apple juice, lime juice, orgeat syrup and apple sauce until smooth.

2. Pour into a chilled lowball glass and sprinkle with cinnamon. Serve immediately.

SANGRÍA SECA

INGREDIENTS

475 ml/16 fl oz tomato juice

225 ml/8 fl oz orange juice

3 measures lime juice

½ measure hot pepper sauce

2 tsp Worcestershire sauce

1 jalapeño chilli, deseeded and finely chopped

celery salt and white pepper

cracked ice cubes

1. Pour the tomato juice, orange juice, lime juice, hot pepper sauce and Worcestershire sauce into a jug

2. Add the chopped chilli and season to taste with the celery salt and white pepper.

3. Stir well, cover and chill in the refrigerator for at least an hour.

4. To serve, half-fill chilled highball glasses with cracked ice and strain the cocktail over it. Serve immediately.

RANCH GIRL

INGREDIENTS

1 measure lime juice

1 measure barbecue sauce

1 dash Worcestershire sauce

1 dash hot pepper sauce

tomato juice

lime slices, to decorate

1 pickled jalapeño chilli,
to decorate

1. Shake the lime juice, barbecue sauce and dashes of Worcestershire sauce and hot pepper sauce over ice cubes until well frosted.

2. Pour into a chilled highball glass, top up with tomato juice and stir.

3. Dress with a couple of slices of lime and a pickled jalapeño chilli. Serve immediately.

NEW ENGLAND PARTY

<<< SERVES 2 >>>

INGREDIENTS

crushed ice
1 dash hot pepper sauce
1 dash Worcestershire sauce
1 tsp lemon juice
1 carrot, chopped
2 celery sticks, chopped
300 ml/10 fl oz tomato juice
150 ml/5 fl oz clam juice
salt and freshly ground black pepper
celery sticks, to decorate

1. Put all the ingredients, except the seasoning and celery stick, into a blender and blend until smooth.

2. Transfer to a jug, cover and chill in the refrigerator for about an hour.

3. Pour into two chilled highball glasses and season to taste.

4. Decorate each glass with a celery stick and serve immediately.

KICK

INDEX

This edition published by Parragon Books Ltd in 2017
LOVE FOOD is an imprint of Parragon Books Ltd

Parragon Books Ltd
Chartist House
15–17 Trim Street
Bath BA1 1HA, UK
www.parragon.co.uk/love-food
www.parragon.com.au/love-food

ISBN 978-1-4748-9725-9

Printed in China

New recipes, introduction and additional text: Michael Stringer
New photography: Mike Cooper
Home economy: Lincoln Jefferson
Cover design: Lexi L'Esteve
Project editor: Emma Clegg

Notes for the Reader
This book uses both metric and imperial measurements. Follow the same units of measurement
throughout; do not mix metric and imperial. All spoon measurements are level: teaspoons are
assumed to be 5 ml, and tablespoons are assumed to be 15 ml.

One measure is assumed to be 25 ml/¾ fl oz. Unless otherwise stated, milk is assumed to be
full fat, eggs and individual fruits and vegetables are medium, pepper is freshly ground black
pepper and salt is table salt.

Images page 8, left and page 9, right, and icons on pages 10-11 used courtesy of iStock.